14
Scriptural Principles
for Daily Living
Vol. 6

14
Scriptural Principles for Daily Living Vol. 6

"Your words are a flashlight to light the path ahead of me and keep me from stumbling."
[Psalm 119:105 TLB]

Anthony Adefarakan

GLOEM, CANADA

CONTENTS

Dedication	1
Acknowledgement	2
Introduction	4
Principle #1 Is it His Will?	7
Principle #2 Is it Banana or Plantain?	10
Principle #3 Why Did Elijah Run?	14
Principle #4 Write Them Down	18

CONTENTS

Principle #5 | You Can Win This Battle — 21

Principle #6 | You Can Frame It — 25

Principle #7 | There is a Place — 28

Principle #8 | Divine Prescription — 31

Principle #9 | I Will Do It Now — 34

Principle #10 | What Will You Call It? — 37

Principle #11 | Did You Know? — 40

Principle #12 | Tell Him As It Is — 42

Principle #13 | It has been the Hegde — 46

CONTENTS

Principle #14 | Never Forget This 50

| Conclusion 54

| WHY YOU REALLY NEED JESUS! 55

| PRAYER POINTS 60

| BECOME A FINANCIAL PARTNER WITH JESUS 61

| About the Author 64

| 67

Dedication

I dedicate this book to God Almighty for His goodness and faithfulness in making His Word available to me. All glory to His Holy Name.

Also to everyone desirous of a closer walk with God, living out His precepts on a daily basis, I am in agreement with you all and I decree that grace for a closer walk with God is coming upon you in Jesus' Name.

Acknowledgement

I sincerely acknowledge my Eternal Father, Who alone is the Source of all wisdom. He is the Author and Finisher of my faith and it is of His fullness that the contents of this book have been drawn.

Also, I want to profoundly appreciate my dear parents – Prince and Mrs. Timothy Adefarakan – for bringing me up in the way of the Lord and for instilling righteousness consciousness in me. The wonderful education foundation I was given, coupled with their constant encouragement has empowered me to reach heights that were once beyond my imagination.

My most special appreciation goes to my sweetheart, Abisolami; without her help and support, I would never have enjoyed the conducive atmosphere needed to publish this book. I appreciate your love, encouragement, and the support you give at all times. Thank you so much. I love you, my Baby!

And to all my mentors in Ministry, I appreciate you all. Your investments in my life are not in vain. May the Lord reward you all in Jesus' Name.

Introduction

Life on earth has been described as a form of pilgrimage with eternity as man's final destination.

1 Peter 2:11 TLB says:
"Dear brothers, you are only visitors here. Since your real home is in heaven, I beg you to keep away from the evil pleasures of this world; they are not for you, for they fight against your very souls."

And Hebrews 11:13 also says:
"These men of faith I have mentioned died without ever receiving all that God had promised them; but they saw it all awaiting them on ahead and were glad, for they agreed that this earth was not their real home but that they were just strangers visiting down here."

In the course of this brief earthly sojourn, we

are bound to face certain situations capable of generating questions like *'what step do I take?' 'where do I settle?' 'who do I marry?' 'will I be rich or poor?' 'how do I finance my projects?' 'how do I take good care of my family?' 'how do I know God's will for my life?'* just to mention a few. Usually, we find it difficult to provide correct answers to these questions due to our weak mortal nature.

However, there is a manual for this pilgrimage, which is the Word of God. The One Who designed this journey for us has put in the manual all we need to navigate our way successfully and to eventually end up on the glorious side of eternity when the pilgrimage is over. Little wonder David prayed in Psalm 119:19 – *"I am a stranger in the earth; hide not thy commandment from me"*.

The principles presented in this Volume 6 are all Bible-based as well and will deliver results every time they are applied because the Word of God is forever settled in Heaven (Psalm 119:89).

I pray as you read on, God's grace to apply these principles will rest upon you in Jesus' Name.

Anthony Adefarakan.

Principle #1

Is it His Will?

Luke 11:9-13 KJV says *"After this manner therefore pray ye: Our Father which art in heaven, Hallowed be thy name. Thy kingdom come. Thy will be done in earth, as it is in heaven.*

Give us this day our daily bread. And forgive us our debts, as we forgive our debtors.

And lead us not into temptation, but deliver us from evil: For thine is the kingdom, and the power, and the glory, for ever. Amen."

Thy will be done on earth... One of the wisest approaches to life is to seek the mind of God at every point in time, whether a year is winding up or a new one is just beginning. This is not just for pastors but for everyone who 'calleth upon the Name of the Lord'.

When entering a New Year for instance, don't just draft out plans of action or New Year resolutions, let God guide you into His will for your life. Remember, He is the One leading you into the New Year, and to Him, the year is not new because He knows the end right from the beginning. He has already finished what you are about to start, so it is a great sign of wisdom to seek His will for the year.

Nothing frustrates a man more than operating outside the will of God. It is the most frustrating way to live. God has a purpose for everything, and that's where His will comes in. What He wants for Brother 'A' may not necessarily be what He wants for Brother 'B'. His purpose is what determines what He allows or disallows in a person's life.

Just imagine a fish (an animal made for the aquatic habitat) praying and making plans to go spend some weeks on land (terrestrial habitat);

how do you think such an adventure will end? Do you think that God will grant the request of that fish if it prayed hard enough? Granting such a request or allowing the fish to go on with its terrestrial plans would simply spell doom for the fish.

Please I encourage you to always check your plans with God through prayers, His Word, and close communion with the Holy Spirit. The safest place to be in the whole world is in the will of God.

Principle #2

Is it Banana or Plantain?

Matthew 7:15-20 NIV says *"Watch out for false prophets. They come to you in sheep's clothing, but inwardly they are ferocious wolves. By their fruit you will recognize them. Do people pick grapes from thornbushes, or figs from thistles? Likewise, every good tree bears good fruit, but a bad tree bears bad fruit. A good tree cannot bear bad fruit, and a bad tree cannot bear good fruit. Every tree that does not bear good fruit is cut down and thrown into the fire. Thus, by their fruit you will recognize them."*

Are Banana and Plantain the same? Have you ever considered how difficult it is to differentiate between banana and plantain plants? Their stems look alike, their leaves look alike, they thrive in the same environment, and sometimes even have similar heights. Quite a number of people have confused banana plant for plantain by merely looking at them. However, there is only one major thing that doesn't look alike in both plants; and that is their "FRUITS". Both plants may generate confusion in the minds of observers for a while, but the moment fruiting commences, all doubts will be gone.

In the same vein, anyone can claim to be a child of God, a Pastor, a Prophet, an Evangelist, a Bishop or even a General Overseer. They may even look like what they claim by carrying big and intimidating Bibles, wearing serious-looking suits, being in charge of big churches with large congregations or some may even be performing unusual miracles; and observers will be persuaded that truly, these men are from God. That is the deception of Plantain and Banana. In order to know which of them is from God, LOOK OUT FOR THEIR FRUITS; NOT THEIR WORKS, TITLES OR

APPEARANCES. Luke 6:43-45 KJV says *"...every tree is known by its own fruit..."* not by its looks.

Matthew 7:21-23 says many people with good works like prophesying, casting out devils among other wonderful works (but without good fruits) will be denied by the Lord Jesus and consequently be shut out of Heaven.

Look at your own life and check if your fruits look like the ones in Galatians 5:22-23 (love, joy, peace, etc); if they are similar, congratulations. With or without any church title or big anointing, your eternity in Heaven is secured. But if your fruits look like those in Galatians 5:19-21 (adultery, fornication, envy, drunkenness, hatred, etc), you are already on your way to Hell regardless of your big church title, anointing, or anything you feel you are doing for God.

Similarly, before you submit your spiritual life to any man or woman of God for mentorship or grooming, watch the fruits at work in their lives. Don't look at the number of people worshiping in their churches or the kinds of miracles they are performing; LOOK FOR THE FRUITS! This is how to be delivered from False Prophets and also be prevented from becoming one yourself. Heaven and Hell are still real! Mark 13:37 CSB says *'And what I say to you, I say to everyone: Be alert!'*

Now you may be asking; 'how then can I begin to bear good fruits?' That's quite simple; just change your ROOTS. Matthew 12:33 says if you make a tree good, the fruits also will become good. Repent of your sinful ways, ask the Lord Jesus (the custodian of good fruits) to come into your life, and start feeding on His Word (the Bible). The fruits will develop, it's GUARANTEED!

Principle #3

Why Did Elijah Run?

1 Kings 19:1-4 NASB says *"Now Ahab told Jezebel all that Elijah had done, and how he had killed all the prophets with the sword. Then Jezebel sent a messenger to Elijah, saying, "So may the gods do to me and even more, if I do not make your life as the life of one of them by tomorrow about this time." And he was afraid and arose and ran for his life and came to Beersheba, which belongs to Judah, and left his servant there. But he himself went a day's journey into the wilderness, and came and sat down under a juniper tree; and he requested for himself that he might die, and said, "It is enough; now, O LORD, take my life, for I am not better than my fathers."*

Why do you think a man who single-handedly

pronounced and executed a death sentence on 450 godless prophets in one day would run away upon hearing a threat from a woman just within 24hours interval? It calls for deep reflection. Many have blamed Elijah for this cowardly move; but if you take a few seconds to do some reflections, you will know why Elijah actually ran.

In the scripture quoted above, we read of king Ahab narrating the Mount Carmel experience which led to the slaughter of the prophets of Baal by Elijah to his (satanic) wife –Jezebel. Upon hearing this report, Jezebel, who had no regard for the God of Israel let alone Elijah, became furious and sent a "message" to Elijah saying by the following day, she was going to kill him just the way he had killed those Baal prophets. Now notice that was a message to be delivered to Elijah, and Elijah was going to hear the message with his ears. The messenger arrived and delivered Jezebel's message to Elijah. Elijah actually heard the message firsthand from the messenger. But the Bible says in verse 3, "And when he (Elijah) saw that, he arose, and went for his life…" Words were spoken to Elijah, but he saw pictures and he ran. This was the same Elijah who had killed 450 powerful Baal prophets just about 24hours ago.

Elijah didn't run because of the message from Jezebel, rather he ran because of what he saw in the process of meditating on what he heard.

It is very important to note that words can become pictures in the mind. Negative words should never be allowed to become pictures (through the process of meditation). The Word of God enjoins us to gird up the loins of our mind (1Peter 1:13). This means we are to take full responsibility for what we allow into our minds as well as what goes on there.

The mere fact that the government announced some foodstuffs as likely breeding grounds for certain disease-causing organisms doesn't mean you will contract a disease if you consume them. It's just a caution.

Also, simply because a particular road has been

described as prone to accidents doesn't mean you shouldn't travel through it or that you should expect to have an accident when you take that road. It's just a report. You don't have to think about everything you hear. Before you meditate or process any words in your mind, they must pass the Philippians 4:8 KJV test: *'Finally, brethren, whatsoever things are true, whatsoever things are honest, whatsoever things are just, whatsoever things are pure, whatsoever things are lovely, whatsoever things are of good report; if there be any virtue, and if there be any praise, think on these things.'* That is the only way to generate positive pictures in your mind.

It is therefore not what you hear that determines your action or reaction; it is what you make out of what you hear. Guard your thoughts!

Principle #4

Write Them Down

Jeremiah 30:1-2 KJV says *"The word that came to Jeremiah from the LORD, saying, Thus speaketh the LORD God of Israel, saying, Write thee all the words that I have spoken unto thee in a book."*

There is something a good number of believers take for granted in relating with God, and it is especially common among Ministers. We go to God in prayers asking Him for revelation or we go into His Word trying to get a message from Him. And when He tells us or shows us something, we just become glad without taking the time to write them down. This is one factor responsible for revelation without corresponding actions which inevitably culminates in lack of desired results.

When God tells you or shows you something, He expects you to get it written (documented). In Jeremiah 30:2 He commanded the prophet to write all He told him in a book; and before He began to show John the Revelator the things to come, He instructed him to write (Revelation 1:19). One of the reasons the Lord doesn't tell or show some of us things is because He knows we won't write them down for necessary action. We just want to feel good with the fact that God speaks to us.

There are two main reasons God wants us to write the things He shows or tells us; firstly, He wants to be quoted. That is, He wants to be used as a reference (Isaiah 46:9-10, 48:3-8). And this is why we keep seeing "it is written" across the entire scriptures. If they had not been written, there would be no reference.

Secondly, He wants to give the future generations opportunity to walk in the light of His Word. Daniel said he understood by books (as documented by prophet Jeremiah) that their captivity in Babylon was not to exceed 70 years and he took the necessary steps to obtain his people's freedom (Daniel 9:2-3; Jeremiah 29:4-10). What if Jeremiah had not written, how would Daniel have run with that vital information? Habakkuk 2:2-3 tells of some visions which are meant for the future generations to run with, and it says they are to be written plainly in order for the readers to run with them.

Please learn to write down the things the Lord reveals to you (for your personal use and if applicable, for the general public), it will give you access to more revelations from Him and the purpose of such revelations will not be defeated. Remember, once revealed, they are no longer secrets (Deuteronomy 29:29, Matthew 10:27). Write them down!

Principle #5

You Can Win This Battle

Deuteronomy 20:1-4 KJV says *"When you go out to battle against your enemies and see horses and chariots and people more numerous than you, do not be afraid of them; for the LORD your God, who brought you up from the land of Egypt, is with you. "When you are approaching the battle, the priest shall come near and speak to the people. "He shall say to them, 'Hear, O Israel, you are approaching the battle against your enemies today. Do not be fainthearted. Do not be afraid, or panic, or tremble before them, for the LORD your God is the one who goes with you, to fight for you against your enemies, to save you.'"*

Are you fighting a battle that seems impossible to win? This is what to do; go back to your previous testimonies. That's where you will find the strength and energy needed to overcome.

Remember David? He needed the courage and energy to defeat a seemingly insurmountable enemy of the entire nation of Israel – Goliath, and all he did was to call to remembrance how God helped him to destroy the bear and the lion that previously attacked him. With that assurance, he simply announced that Goliath (the present battle) would be like one of them (the previous battles). And guess what? That was exactly what happened; he (though a lad) defeated a well experienced and fully armed giant (Goliath).

1 Samuel 17:32-37 NASB gives the account: *'David said to Saul, "Let no man's heart fail on account of him; your servant will go and fight with this Philistine." Then Saul said to David, "You are not able to go against this Philistine to fight with him;*

for you are but a youth while he has been a warrior from his youth."

But David said to Saul, "Your servant was tending his father's sheep. When a lion or a bear came and took a lamb from the flock, I went out after him and attacked him, and rescued it from his mouth; and when he rose up against me, I seized him by his beard and struck him and killed him. "Your servant has killed both the lion and the bear; and this uncircumcised Philistine will be like one of them, since he has taunted the armies of the living God." And David said, "The LORD who delivered me from the paw of the lion and from the paw of the bear, He will deliver me from the hand of this Philistine." And Saul said to David, "Go, and may the LORD be with you."

And by the time you get to verses 48-51, Goliath was declared dead.

Nothing arms a man for current battles more than the strength drawn from past victories. Our opening text says the children of Israel needed to remember the Lord their God Who brought them out of the land of Egypt (the land of their generational captivity) for them to overcome their current battle without fear.

Jonah 2:7 says when my soul fainted within me, I remembered the Lord. And that's what David did. He remembered the Lord: he said *'the Lord who delivered me from the bear and the lion would deliver me from this Goliath.'*

In other words, he was saying 'the Lord Who gave me victory in my previous battles will give me victory in this current one'. And that's what the Lord did.
Do the same, the God of David has not changed a bit (Malachi 3:6; Hebrews 13:8). Praise God!

Principle #6

You Can Frame It

John 1:1-5 KJV says *"In the beginning was the Word, and the Word was with God, and the Word was God. The same was in the beginning with God. All things were made by him; and without him was not any thing made that was made. In him was life; and the life was the light of men. And the light shineth in darkness; and the darkness comprehended it not."*

Verse 1a says *"In the beginning was the Word..."* That is, nothing existed until the Word was in place; and even if anything will still exist now, it will have to be by the Word. This implies that for anything you plan embarking upon, you must get a Word for it right at the beginning. No starting until there is a Word.

For instance, as you begin a new year, a career, a business, a new family, a new journey, a ministry, an appointment, projects, a new week, a new day, etc, you must have a Word to stand on. According to Genesis 1:1 and John 1:1, it was actually the Word Who created the heavens and the earth. Hebrews 11:3 says the whole world (that we see now) was framed by the Word of God. So, in order to create your dreams, desires, and any other thing you intend to see manifest in your life, you need the Word to frame it. To God's glory, I have enjoyed Divine Health for several years now simply because of the knowledge of Jesus Christ as the Vine and I as a branch connected to Him (John 15:5). That's what framed my Health world.

As you enter a new year, get into the Bible, and receive a Word by which your year will be framed. In our ministry, the Lord gave us a Word in the year 2017 that *'we are breaking new grounds and no man shall be able to stand before us'* (Joshua 1:3-5); we received it, gave thanks for it, and expected it to frame our operations. That Word came as we were about entering 2017, and by the December of that same year, the Lord opened a door of ministry for us in North America. By December 2018, our ministry was registered in Canada and the Lord has been enlarging our coasts since then. According to the Word we received, we actually broke new grounds and no man was able to stand before us (no opposition whatsoever). That is how to use the Word of God to frame your life and operations.

For reading this today, I have a Word for you; if you will believe and say 'Amen', "This very week, the Lord will bless you, and He will surround you with favour as with a shield" – Psalm 5:12.
Shalom!

Principle #7

There is a Place

Revelation 20:11-15 NIV says *"Then I saw a great white throne and him who was seated on it. The earth and the heavens fled from his presence, and there was no place for them. And I saw the dead, great and small, standing before the throne, and books were opened. Another book was opened, which is the book of life. The dead were judged according to what they had done as recorded in the books. The sea gave up the dead that were in it, and death and Hades gave up the dead that were in them, and each person was judged according to what they had done. Then death and Hades were thrown into the lake of fire. The lake of fire is the second death. Anyone whose name was not found written in the book of life was thrown into the lake of fire."*

There is a place; it is a place of unending tears, crying, sorrow, and torment. The occupants of this place groan in regrets because of the opportunities they had wasted, the wrong decisions they had made, and also the bad choices they had embraced.

In this place, both great and small are subjected to the same treatment of intense pain and agony. As a matter of fact, in this particular place, Politicians, Bishops, Pastors, Prostitutes, Armed robbers, Assassins, Civil servants, Presidents of nations, Kings, Messengers etc have the same fate of perpetual suffering.

There is more to this place, none of the occupants has the opportunity to escape the aforementioned experiences; not even through death. It is a cup they must fully drink.

To belong to this place is not difficult at all, you only need to intensify the rate at which you tell lies, cheat, fornicate and gossip. Also, you will need to commit adultery the more as well as idolatry. Just keep living in total disobedience to all of God's instructions for living (the Bible), and you will soon join the people there (though that's neither God's desire nor my desire for you).

However, if your decision is to never find yourself there, you only have one task to carry out. You must URGENTLY REPENT OF ALL YOUR SINS AND CALL ON THE LORD JESUS CHRIST TO SAVE YOUR SOUL. He is the only Way out of this terrible place (John 14:6). If you follow Him, you will never be lost. The place is called Hell (eternal damnation). Act Now and Act Fast, people go to Hell daily. Please let others also know about this, it is a place you will not wish for even your enemies.

Principle #8

Divine Prescription

Ephesians 4:30-32 (TLB) says *"Don't cause the Holy Spirit sorrow by the way you live. Remember, he is the one who marks you to be present on that day when salvation from sin will be complete.*

Stop being mean, bad-tempered, and angry. Quarreling, harsh words, and dislike of others should have no place in your lives. Instead, be kind to each other, tenderhearted, forgiving one another, just as God has forgiven you because you belong to Christ."

These are the ways the Lord expects His children to live.

Don't cause the Holy Spirit sorrow by the

way you live... The Holy Spirit is the One living in you and constantly prompting you to act in accordance with the will of God. He constantly tells you the right things to do and the wrong things to avoid. If you keep disobeying His promptings, you are actually causing Him sorrow by the way you live. When He tells you to say the truth and you choose to tell lies, He is not happy. And even though He is a very patient Spirit, if you keep causing Him sorrow by not following His leadings, He will become frustrated and stop talking to you. He will simply leave you alone. And when that happens, not only will you become exposed to satanic attacks, you also stand the risk of ending up in hell because according to our opening text, it is the Holy Spirit who marks you to be present on that day when salvation from sin will be complete. Don't grieve Him anymore; the consequences are so grievous.

The other part of that prescription says ***"Stop being mean, bad-tempered, and angry. Quarreling, harsh words, and dislike of others should have no place in your lives. Instead, be kind*** *to each other, tenderhearted, forgiving one another, just as God has forgiven you because you belong to Christ."*

The Lord wants you to be kind and not to be quarrelsome. And one of the ways He wants you to do this is by forgiving other people the same way God forgave you because of your connection with Christ. That is, because you were forgiven for Christ's sake, He expects you to also forgive others for Christ's sake (whether you think they deserve it or not, because you too didn't deserve His forgiveness).

Think about these principles and align yourself to live by them; that way, you will be pleasing God.

Principle #9

I Will Do It Now

Ezekiel 12:28 (TLB) says *"Therefore say to them: 'The Lord God says: All delay has ended! I will do it now!'"*

This principle is prophetic in dimension and I will like you to connect your spirit to receive what the Lord is telling you through it.

Abraham had a delay before he experienced the fulfillment of God's promise.

Sarah had a delay before she became a joyful mother.

Hannah had a delay before she became pregnant.

Isaac had a delay before becoming a father.

Rebecca had a delay before she could bear children.

Rachel had a delay before becoming a mother.

Moses had a delay before commencing his ministry.

Joseph had a delay before the fulfillment of his dreams.

The Israelites had a delay before leaving Egypt for Canaan.

Elizabeth had a delay before conceiving a child.

Zechariah had a delay before becoming a father.

David had a delay before he could ascend his throne.

All these were covenant people, yet they tasted

some forms of delay before their expectations came to pass.

But the Lord asked me to tell you this concerning His promises, prophecies, and your long-awaited expectations: ***"All delay has ended! I will do it now!"*** (Ezekiel 12:28 TLB).

And for as many who will believe this message from the Lord, I will like to further announce to you that you should expect the first performance of it this very month according to Luke 1:45.

However, remember that the Lord expects you to testify to His goodness as soon as He confirms His Word in your life. Please make sure you do.

There shall be a Performance! Congratulations! Now go ahead and give Him praise for this Word. Praise the Lord!

Principle #10

What Will You Call It?

Genesis 2:19 KJV *says "And out of the ground the LORD God formed every beast of the field, and every fowl of the air; and brought them unto Adam to see what he would call them: and whatsoever Adam called every living creature, that was the name thereof."*

The Lord God created some animals and brought them to Adam to see what he would call them. And it was recorded that whatever Adam called them became their names (without any form of interference from God).

In the same vein, the Lord consciously allows some circumstances to come our way just to see what we will call them. And just as He didn't interfere with Adam's discretion back then, He may not change whatever you call your own.

As a child of God, you will have to learn to use the power of your tongue to your own advantage. Don't call that thing troubling your belly stomach ache or fibroid if you are in need of a child, rather call it 'baby is kicking' and it shall be so. You have just received a note from your Landlord and you are panicking because they wrote 'eviction notice' on it. Stop panicking, call it 'my letter of promotion to become a Landlord' and you will be surprised at how things will turn out.

Always remember this: There is no situation that has its own name, they only bear the names we give to them. Cancer is being called cancer today because we named it cancer. Disappointment is being called this name because someone named it 'disappointment'. There are no bad news anywhere, the only ones you will likely find are the ones people have named bad news. Every situation will only bear the name(s) we give to them. And that's where the disciplined use of our tongue comes in.

"YOUR CONFESSION IN THE TIME OF YOUR CONFUSION IS THE CONCLUSION OF YOUR CONDITION". Think about that!

Principle #11

Did You Know?

Colossians 2:9-10 KJV says *"For in him dwelleth all the fulness of the Godhead bodily. And ye are complete in him, which is the head of all principality and power:"*

Have you really considered and grasped the implication of this text that says Christ is the Head of all principality and power? Have you?

Demonic forces have hierarchies just like human soldiers. They have senior and junior officers, and their tasks are based on their ranks. Among these dark forces, principalities and powers rank as very senior officers. You can confirm this in Ephesians 6:12. They are very wicked. Yet the Word of the Lord says Christ (the One you received at

Salvation Who now lives in you) is the Head of ALL PRINCIPALITY AND POWER. This simply means all these forces cannot carry out a single operation anywhere without the knowledge and permission of the Head. He will have to allow them before they can operate anywhere. And if you have surrendered your life to Him (Christ, their Head), you can be sure He will never grant them permission to afflict you.

Running from witches and wizards is a clear sign of insanity if you are in Christ. These are very junior officers in the kingdom of darkness. They are like messengers with very low ranks. And if principalities and powers (chief officers) shake and tremble before the Head, they dare not near you if you are in Christ. The Lord laid this on my heart to share with you and I have just done so.

Please kindly find your place in Christ, understand your privileges, and start behaving like someone who really knows. It shall be well with you.

Principle #12

Tell Him As It Is

Hebrews 4:14-16 KJV says *"Seeing then that we have a great high priest, that is passed into the heavens, Jesus the Son of God, let us hold fast our profession. For we have not an high priest which cannot be touched with the feeling of our infirmities; but was in all points tempted like as we are, yet without sin. Let us therefore come boldly unto the throne of grace, that we may obtain mercy, and find grace to help in time of need."*

Once you surrender your life to Jesus Christ, you can afford to be very open with Him. You are free to tell Him exactly how you feel in your body, concerning your job, about your marriage etc. The Lord wants to fix everything that needs to be fixed in your life because He feels what you feel and wants you comfortable.

Isaiah 63:9 NIV says *'In all their distress he too was distressed, and the angel of his presence saved them. In his love and mercy he redeemed them; he lifted them up and carried them all the days of old.'*

When you are not fine the Lord is not fine too. He loves you that much. Our opening text says the Lord is touched by our feeling of infirmities; He knows and feels exactly what we are experiencing.

In fact, something interesting happened in Acts 9:1-6 KJV during the conversion of Saul on the road to Damascus: *'And Saul, yet breathing out threatenings and slaughter against the disciples of the Lord, went unto the high priest, And desired of him letters to Damascus to the synagogues, that if he found any of this way, whether they were men or women, he might bring them bound unto Jerusalem. And as he journeyed, he came near Damascus: and suddenly there shined round about him a light from heaven: And he fell to the earth, and heard a voice saying unto him, Saul, Saul, why persecutest thou me? And he said, Who art thou, Lord? And the Lord said, I am Jesus whom thou persecutest: it is hard for thee to kick against the pricks. And he trembling and astonished said, Lord, what wilt thou have me to do? And the Lord said unto him, Arise, and go into the city, and it shall be told thee what thou must do.'*

Saul had never seen or met Jesus Christ before, he was only persecuting those who believed in Him – the Christians. But when Jesus Christ appeared to Him on this very day of his conversion, He asked him: *'Why are you persecuting Me?* And when Saul asked Who He was, He introduced Himself as the Jesus he has been persecuting.

Did you see that? Saul was persecuting the Church, but Jesus was also feeling persecuted. That's because He feels whatever we feel. And because of that connection, He knows the best way to end our sufferings. It is when we feel alright that He feels alright too.

With this understanding, kindly be free to come before Him and tell Him everything you are passing through. Tell Him as it is because He understands. That is one of the privileges of being a child of God. Begin to use your privileges today and you will be mightily blessed.

Principle #13

It has been the Hegde

Job 1:6-10 KJV says *"Now there was a day when the sons of God came to present themselves before the LORD, and Satan came also among them. And the LORD said unto Satan, Whence comest thou? Then Satan answered the LORD, and said, From going to and fro in the earth, and from walking up and down in it. And the LORD said unto Satan, Hast thou considered my servant Job, that there is none like him in the earth, a perfect and an upright man, one that feareth God, and escheweth evil? Then Satan answered the LORD, and said, Doth Job fear God for nought? Hast not thou made an hedge about him, and about his house, and about all that he hath on every side? thou hast blessed the work of his hands, and his substance is increased in the land."*

You hear about all the evil happenings around you but none of them befalls you, you succeed where others fail, you survived what killed others, you enjoy sound health in the midst of a pandemic, you are financially blessed in the midst of economic hardship etc. These are not as a result of your righteousness, fasting or vigil, neither do they imply that the devil didn't make efforts at destroying you; all you have simply enjoyed is the HEDGE of the Lord.

The devil gave us a very important revelation in Job 1:9; he said he couldn't attack Job because of the Hedge the Lord surrounded him with. That is exactly what you are also enjoying. It has been the Hedge. In agriculture, a hedge can be described as a fence or boundary formed by closely growing bushes or shrubs. It simply prevents any unwanted animals from gaining access into a garden or a plantation. The purpose of this hedge is to protect what is planted.

Isaiah 61:3 says you are the planting of the Lord; and that explains why He surrounds you with His Hedge. I feel you should spend quality time daily thanking God for His Hedge over your life and all that you own.

Now, it is important to note that as beautiful as this Hedge is, it is only meant for God's people – those who are on His side. Job was described as a righteous man, that's why he had the Hedge around his life. You too will have to remain righteous in order to keep enjoying the Lord's Hedge. The moment sin sets in, the Hedge can no longer hold until the sin is addressed and the Hedge is rebuilt. The devil has been described as a serpent in the Bible; and according to Ecclesiastes 10:8 KJV, *'...whoso breaketh an hedge, a serpent shall bite him.'* That means, if you break the Hedge (by sinning), you will be exposed to Satan's attack.

So, thank God for the Hedge, but ensure the Hedge doesn't get broken so as not to forfeit your security.

14 SCRIPTURAL PRINCIPLES FOR DAILY LIVING
VOL. 6

Principle #14

Never Forget This

1 Corinthians 10:13 NKJV *says "No temptation has overtaken you except such as is common to man; but God is faithful, who will not allow you to be tempted beyond what you are able, but with the temptation will also make the way of escape, that you may be able to bear it."*

What you are passing through must never paint God as unfaithful. As a matter of fact, it is His faithfulness that will bring you out of the mess you are currently in.

Let's examine the faithfulness of God for a moment.

The Bible says God is love according to 1 John

4:8. But it also says He hates iniquity (Hebrews 1:9). So what motivated Him to send His Son to die for sinners (those involved in what He hates)? The answer is found in that same 1 John 4:8, He is Love. His love for sinners is greater than His hatred for sin. That's why Romans 5:8 NIV says *'But God demonstrates his own love for us in this: While we were still sinners, Christ died for us'* and John 3:16-17 KJV confirms it: *'For God so loved the world, that he gave his only begotten Son, that whosoever believeth in him should not perish, but have everlasting life. For God sent not his Son into the world to condemn the world; but that the world through him might be saved.'*

God is love, and there's nothing you can do to change that about Him. He will keep loving even when all He gets back is hatred and hostility.

2 Timothy 2:11-13 KJV says *'This is a faithful saying: For if we died with Him, We shall also live with Him. If we endure, We shall also reign with Him. If we deny Him, He also will deny us.*

If we are faithless, He remains faithful; He cannot deny Himself.'

Did you see that? If we are faithless, He will remain faithful because He cannot deny Himself. He can't change His nature just because of our faithlessness.

That's why if you promise to do something for Him and you fail to do it, He will not be happy with you and may even deal with you at some point; but that doesn't mean He won't wake you up the next morning or deny you your daily bread. He will keep doing what His faithfulness demands regardless of your own unfaithfulness.

Check out the characteristics of God's kind of love (agape) as described in 1 Corinthians 13:1-8; you will have an idea about why He does what He does.

So if you are in trouble and He has promised to deliver you (or make a way of escape for you), you can be rest assured that He will do just that.

Numbers 23:19 KJV *says 'God is not a man, that he should lie; neither the son of man, that he should repent: hath he said, and shall he not do it? or hath he spoken, and shall he not make it good?'*

God is always faithful, please NEVER FORGET THAT!

Conclusion

So far, the Lord has revealed some biblical principles to us. The purpose is not just to know, document or preach them, rather they were revealed so that we can walk in them.

According to John 8:32, only the truth that is known sets free. So, go through these principles one by one and determine to build your Christian walk around them for a life of Kingdom impact here on earth.

Jesus said in John 13:17(NLT) - *"You know these things- now do them! That is the path of blessing."*

May the Lord release upon you and your entire household the grace to walk worthy of His calling upon your lives in Jesus' Name!

WHY YOU REALLY NEED JESUS!

You might have heard a lot of Preachers talk about the importance of surrendering one's life to Jesus and even the dangers of not doing so at one time or the other without you being really moved. But with these three (3) important reasons highlighted below, I strongly believe you will not need another sermon before deciding to yield to His saving grace regardless of your religious beliefs.

1. **You have an Enemy to overcome:** There is an adversary who is all out to steal from you, kill you and destroy you regardless of your level of education, moral uprightness, societal influence or even religious beliefs. He is Devil by name (John 10:10, 1 Peter 5: 8), and he doesn't release any of

his captives until he completely destroys their souls in hell. The ONLY One Who can deliver you from his manipulations and also save your soul from him is Jesus Christ.

2. **You have an Appointment to keep:** Being alive and reading this implies you have a very important and inevitable appointment to keep. It is an appointment with death (Hebrews 9:27). Death is the sure end of all mortals (of which you are part); and to enable you prepare for this appointment without fear of eternal damnation, you need Jesus. He is the ONLY One Who has power over death (Revelation 1:18).

3. **You have a Judge to face:** Upon departure from this earth, you will have to stand before a judgment throne to render an account of your earthly life (Hebrews 9:27, Romans 14:12). The outcome of this judgment is what will determine your eternal abode which will either be Heaven

or the Lake of fire. Interestingly, the Judge Who will preside over your case and also decide where you will spend your eternity is Jesus (John 5:21-30, 2 Timothy 4:1). I perceive you are thinking "is God not our Judge? Why Jesus?' Well, you are not wrong. But God the Father Himself is the One Who handed over all the judgment to His Son, Jesus Christ. Read verse 22 of that John chapter 5. So Jesus is the ONLY One Who has the power to either judge you guilty or guiltless in eternity.

Now that you know these, the wisest thing you can do for yourself is to quickly establish a relationship with Jesus, since you don't even know how close your appointment with death is. To do this, say this prayer aloud:

"Lord Jesus, I am a sinner and I cannot help myself. Wash me in your precious blood and make me a new creature. I open the door of my heart to you today, come into my life and become my Lord and Savior. Grant me the grace

to overcome the devil, prepare me for eternity and help me to escape the judgment reserved for sinners. Thank You Jesus for saving me. Amen."

Congratulations! You are now SAVED. Go and sin no more.

To learn more about your new relationship with Jesus, kindly send an Email to info@gloem.org or emancipation4souls@yahoo.com, we will send you a material that will help you. You can also call, text or send a WhatsApp message to +1 587 9735910 or +1 587 9695910 for further assistance.

And to learn more about God, His Word and His plans for your life, kindly visit our Facebook page [***https://www.facebook.com/gloem.org***] for daily meditation in the Word of God (all year round) and our Blog page [***https://gloem.org/myblog***] for life-transforming publications.

You are also invited to listen to Freedom Podcast: The Official Weekly Podcast of Global Emancipation Ministries – Calgary via https://anchor.fm/gloem

All these great resources capable of developing your spiritual stamina will help you become an overcomer in life regardless of what comes your way.

PRAYER POINTS

1. Father, thank You for opening my eyes to the truths contained in this book.
2. Father, please cause every experience in my life to work together for my good.
3. I cancel everything that is working against my spiritual growth in Jesus' Name.
4. God of all possibilities, please cause my grass to become green again.
5. From today, my testimonies shall no longer be delayed in Jesus' Name.
6. Father, beginning from now, please release upon me and my household the ability to walk with you and serve you faithfully in the Name of Jesus.
7. Father, I thank You for answering all my prayers. Glory be to Your Holy Name. Hallelujah!

BECOME A FINANCIAL PARTNER WITH JESUS

At *Global Emancipation Ministries - Calgary*, our mandate is *to liberate men through the knowledge of the Truth* and our mission statement is *creating channels through which men can encounter the Truth - [Isaiah 61:1-3; John 8:32, 36; I Thessalonians 5:24]*.

Our Ministerial Activities include Rural and Urban Evangelical Outreaches, Prison Evangelism, Hospital Ministrations, Mobilization for Missions Support, Teaching of the undiluted Word of God, Scripture-Based Seminars, Discipleship, Training of Field Missionaries and Empowerment of underprivileged ones among other Field Ministerial Tasks.

If you sense the Lord is calling you to reach out to the lost by engaging in any of these activities or by assisting those involved with your resources, please feel free to join us. Let us come together as we take the Gospel of our Lord Jesus Christ to the hurting and forgotten ones. [Mark 16:15-20].

Please join us in these kingdom projects by making your weekly, monthly, quarterly, or annual donations to Global Emancipation Ministries – Calgary.

You can visit the "GIVE" section on our website, www.gloem.org, to learn about the ways to give.

For acknowledgement, please advise your donations to us by email: info@gloem.org or emancipation4souls@yahoo.com, and kindly include your details i.e. name, address, email and location. Alternatively, you can simply call +1 587 9735910 to do same.

You can also volunteer your gifts and talents in the service of the Lord through our ministerial platforms regardless of your location. To get information on how to go about this, please visit www.gloem.org and contact us via email: info@gloem.org or emancipation4souls@yahoo.com.

God bless you.

About the Author

By the special grace of God, **Anthony O. Adefarakan** is the privileged President of **Global Emancipation Ministries - Calgary (GLOEM)** with headquarters in Canada, North America, and **Emancipating Truth Ministry International (ETMI)** with headquarters in Nigeria, West Africa.

The Lord called him into the field ministry in February 2008 with the mandate to liberate men through the knowledge of the Truth, and by December 2012 he was ordained and commissioned as the Pioneer Pastor – in – Charge of The Redeemed Christian Church of God, Revelation Parish, Shalom Area under Delta Province III, Nigeria where he served until 1st February 2015 when he officially handed over to a new Pastor in order to focus on his field ministry to which the Lord had earlier called him and for which the authority of the church had already prayed and released him to undertake.

On 29th September 2013, he was awarded a Post Graduate Diploma in Tent – Making Mission from the Redeemed Christian School of Missions, Nigeria (RECSOM, Asaba Campus) where he also had the privilege to train Pastors and Missionaries as a lecturer in 2017.

Since the commissioning of his field ministry in 2015 he has had the opportunity to lead his ministry officers to field ministrations in different Prisons, Hospitals, Orphanages, Rural communities, Camp settlements, Markets, Local churches among other places with great successes on all occasions – such as the salvation of sinners, healing

ANTHONY ADEFARAKAN

of the sick, financial empowerment of mission churches, provision of relief materials to the poor, provision of medical services to the underprivileged, baptism in the Holy Ghost, deliverance from demonic oppression, the release of inmates just to mention a few - all to the glory of God Who alone is the Doer.

He is the author of other best-selling titles such as *The Law of Kinds, Learning From the Ants, The Immutability of God's Counsel, Surely there is an End, Life Applicable lessons from the Book of Ruth, One thing is Needful Weekly Devotional Guide, Life Applicable Revelations from God's Word* **(Volumes 1 and 2)** among others.

He is blissfully married to Ifeoluwa A. Adefarakan and their marriage is fruitful to the glory of God.

Jesus is his Message, Freedom is the Outcome! Isaiah 61:1-3

www.ingramcontent.com/pod-product-compliance
Lightning Source LLC
Chambersburg PA
CBHW021431070526
44577CB00001B/158